BRUCE LEE

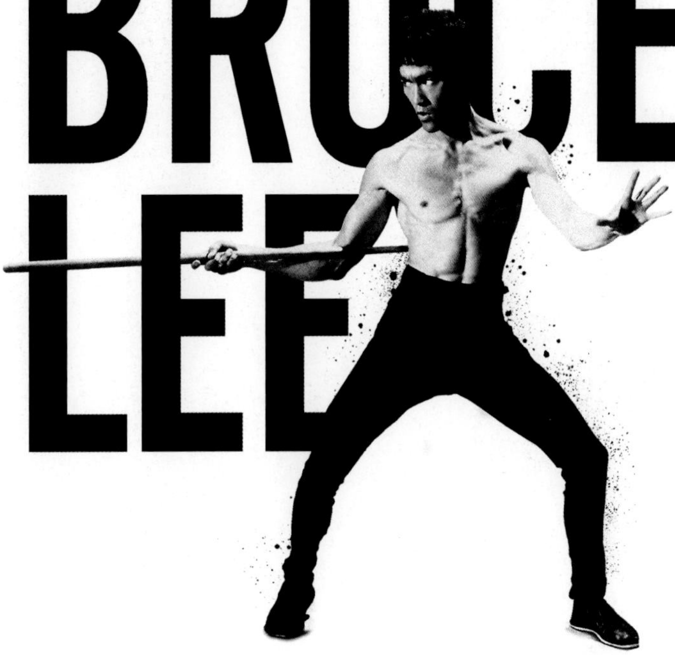

THIS IS A CARLTON BOOK

Published by Carlton Books Limited
20 Mortimer Street
London W1T 3JW

A CIP catalogue for this book is available from the British Library.

ISBN 978-1-78097-694-5

Printed in Dubai

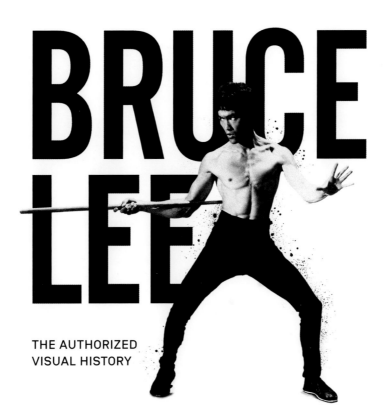

BRUCE LEE

THE AUTHORIZED VISUAL HISTORY

STEVE KERRIDGE

FOREWORD BY
SHANNON LEE

CARLTON
BOOKS

CONTENTS

FOREWORD
BY SHANNNON LEE
6

INTRODUCTION
8

01
CHILDHOOD AND TEENAGE YEARS 1940–59
12

02
EVOLUTION 1960–71
30

03

THE HOLLYWOOD YEARS 1965–70

70

04

HONG KONG 1970–73

100

FOREWORD

BY SHANNON LEE

I often tell people that the true magic and power of Bruce Lee is that he knew who he was, and he lived his life to the fullest. And the magic and power of that is that we all can do that too. My father was a cultivated and practiced man who worked hard and never stopped researching his own experience. And the beautiful thing about him was that he shared his results with all of us in a fun, entertaining (and often profound) way. His mere image exudes his energy.

I feel secure in the knowledge that there will never be another Bruce Lee because there simply can't be. He was so himself quintessentially and purely, and we are all better for him having pursued his path. So while this may seem like a picture book with some biographical information, it in actuality is a gateway into excellence, unrelenting self-work and love. Yes, love. Because Bruce Lee loved life.

Shannon Lee, Los Angeles, 2017

INTRODUCTION

BY STEVE KERRIDGE

TO CONDENSE A LIFE SO FULL AS THAT OF BRUCE LEE INTO A SINGLE BOOK OF IMAGES IS EASIER SAID THAN DONE. UPON BEING CONTACTED BY THE BRUCE LEE ESTATE IN LOS ANGELES IN EARLY 2016, I BEGAN, AFTER MUCH DELIBERATION, THE MAMMOTH TASK OF CURATING PHOTOGRAPHS TO SHOW THE LIFE OF BRUCE LEE.

To relay his life to another aficionado of Bruce Lee would be straightforward, but the realization that I would be facing the general public, who wouldn't know too much about this iconic figure, would be the comparative distinction between Albert Einstein talking math to fellow mathematicians, or him trying to explain quantum physics to the general public. Following several meetings with the publisher, I began to envisage a compact yet comprehensive volume that would educate the reader on the life of Bruce Lee through the visual medium. As the title of this book suggests, Bruce's life took place around a visual framework of photography that acts as a time capsule in an age long gone. From the war, and post-war streets of Hong Kong, the new age of the 1950s, the counter-cultural 1960s and finally the early 1970s, when pop culture went mainstream, we can see this young man grow and develop into the most influential martial artist and action movie star that ever lived.

Everybody that grew up in the 1970s will remember the impact Bruce Lee had on youth culture. It seemed that everybody was learning 'Kung Fu' and that every church hall and social club was a venue for martial art classes.

In late 1973, as a child aged ten, I found myself staring at the image on a cover of a magazine in my local newsagent. An old book my father had given me several years earlier, entitled *The Manual of Karate* by E.J. Harrison, led me to assume the image of this man on the magazine cover was demonstrating Karate. The man, of course, was Bruce Lee, and I was totally mesmerized. I had never heard of Bruce Lee, let alone know that he had passed away several months previously. I went home and told my mother what I had seen. To my surprise, later that day she walked into my room and handed me the magazine. I was hooked from then onwards, and to me Bruce Lee seemed as much a 'Superman' as the one who wore his underwear on the outside of his trousers and a giant 'S' on his chest.

Ever since that day in 1973, the fascination and intrigue I have held for Bruce Lee has never ceased. I began studying martial arts, and I still do, teaching it, breathing it and totally living it to this day due to this icon that didn't live long enough to see the huge influence he made upon the world.

I suppose we can all agree on the fact that certain individuals have made a unique impact upon the citizens of this world – Elvis, the Beatles, James Dean, Marilyn Monroe, etc. Bruce Lee certainly falls into this category. He influenced moviemakers, producers, directors and actors alike. He re-invented the martial mind by giving people the freedom of thought, to break away from conformity and ritual, or as he put it best – "the Classical Mess". The modern trend of mixed martial arts is only what Bruce Lee was doing some 50-plus years ago, before anyone else dared step outside the box.

His philosophical approach, not only to martial arts but also to life, has had a profound influence on many people. Bruce Lee, as you will observe within these pages, was an ever-changing, ever-evolving individual who believed in individuality and expressing oneself, which really is the basis of his martial art concept of Jeet Kune Do.

Compiling this book, with help along the way from my fellow Bruce Lee historian Greg Rhodes, certainly had many challenges. I had to provide guidance for the correct photographic material, and it was most difficult to keep the photograph count down enough to fit into a single volume of work.

After much thought, Greg and I decided to arrange the book into chapters that would cover his childhood and teenage years for the 1940s and 1950s, and the evolution of his martial art and Hollywood during the 1960s. The 1970s would complete his years in Hong Kong between 1971 and 1973 and his movies made at Golden Harvest.

This book should be seen with the view of celebrating a man who lived his life without boundaries, a man that created his own circumstances. Bruce Lee was certainly a movie star, but more a martial artist first, and I hope the reader will get a fuller appreciation of this legend and his legendary journey.

I mentioned earlier how as a ten-year-old child, I viewed Bruce Lee as a 'Superman'. Now, some 40-plus years later, I realize he became what he wanted to be described as since the beginning – a 'Super' human being.

Steve Kerridge, London 2017

CHAPTER

01

CHILDHOOD
AND TEENAGE
YEARS 1940–59

Lee Jun-Fan was born to Chinese parents in San Francisco on November 27, 1940. It was the year of the Dragon. The entire family moved back to Hong Kong in March 1941, and it was during school holidays from La Salle College that a young Lee would visit his father, Lee Hoi-Chuen, at work on movie sets. Throughout the next 18 years, Bruce would go on have small roles in 18 movies, *The Orphan* (1958) being the most notable and critically acclaimed. Unlike his older siblings who were more inclined toward scholarship, Bruce was more extroverted and outgoing, often seeking diversion and entertainment outside the security and sanctity of the family home. William Cheung, who had met Lee through a neighbourhood friend, happened to practice Wing Chun Gung Fu, and so introduced Lee to the famous Sifu, Yip Man. Bruce was a keen student, but on April 29, 1959, an 18-year old Bruce Lee boarded the U.S.S. *President Wilson* to return to the United States of America.

Clockwise, from top left:

Baby Bruce in San Francisco.

Bruce's parents, Grace Lee and Lee Hoi-Chuen.

Bruce alongside Peter, Phoebe and Agnes.

Grace Lee and Lee Hoi-Chuen with their children, Bruce, Peter, Phoebe and Agnes.

A proud Lee Hoi-Chuen, holding up his newly born son for the camera, with stage make-up on Bruce.

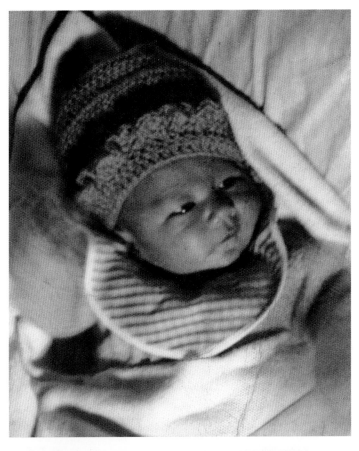

Left: A young Bruce alongside brother Peter, with family friend.

Above: Bruce and Peter playing with toy swords.

Right: A young Bruce posing for the camera during a family day out.

Below: La Salle Primary School class photo with Bruce, second row down, second from left.

> **EVER SINCE I WAS A CHILD I HAVE HAD THIS INSTINCTIVE URGE FOR EXPANSION AND GROWTH.**
>
> *Bruce Lee*

Left: A family children group photo. From left to right: Agnes, Robert, Peter (top), Bruce (bottom), one of the cousins from China, and Phoebe.

Above: Family group photo with Bruce centre, including various aunts, uncles and cousins.

Right: A publicity photo with a young Bruce kneeling centre alongside Hong Kong Cantonese opera actress Hung Sin-Nui from the 1953 movie *A Mother's Tears*.

Left: Publicity photo from the 1955 movie *Love Part One and Part Two*.

Above: An example of life imitating art with a knife-wielding Bruce in *Kid Cheung*.

Above right: La Salle Secondary School class photo (Bruce, seventh from right, back row).

Right: St Francis Xavier School class photo. Bruce, second row from bottom, third from left.

"GO BRAVELY ON MY FRIEND, BECAUSE EACH NEW EXPERIENCE TEACHES US A LESSON. "

Bruce Lee

Far Left and Left: Bruce with Yip Man, 1957.

Below: Bruce's decription of the photo.

Bottom: Gung Fu practice with close family friend, Wu Ngan Jai.

The great master of
Wing Chung Gung Fu.
Mr. Yip Man.

Taken in
15 sept. 1957

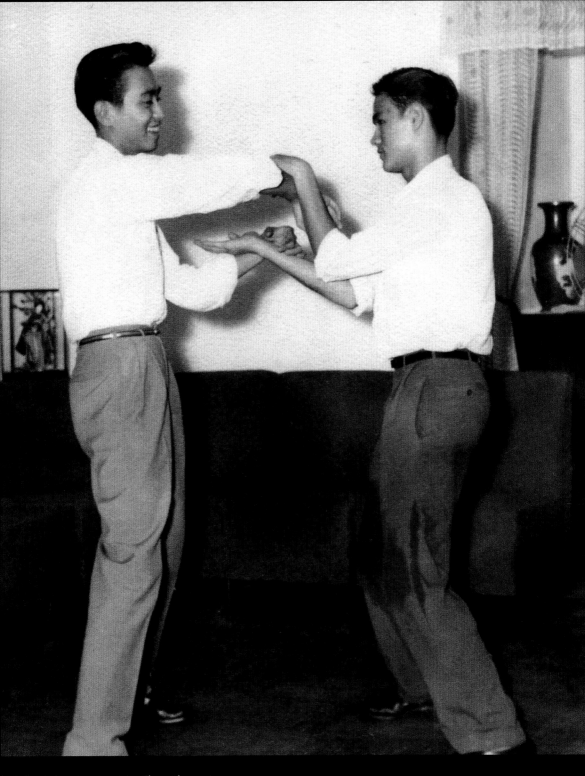

Left and Above: Practising Wing Chun with a cousin.

Overleaf: Bruce in dubbing studio, standing with cast and crew of
Thunderstorm (1957).

Above left and right: Bruce with dance partner Margaret Leung practicing the Cha-Cha.

Below: Bruce's personal notebook showing the Cha-Cha moves.

Opposite page: A photo from *The Orphan* (1958).

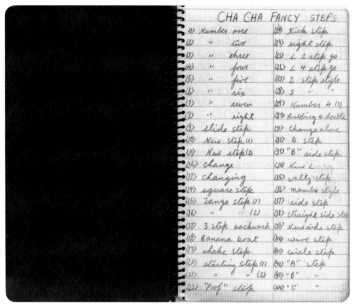

CHA CHA FANCY STEPS

(1) Number one	(23) Kick step	(68) 4 break step	三月初一 (MARY)
(2) " two	(24) eight step	(69) single step	七月十一 (PEARL)
(3) " three	(25) L 2 step go	(70) 3 counts	六月初四 (HOWARD)
(4) " four	(26) L 4 step go	(71) without counts	二月初二 (MRS TSO)
(5) " five	(27) 2 step style	(72) break step	九月十五 (MR. ")
(6) " six	(28) 3 "	(73) rt. L. step.	七月初九 (PO WING)
(7) " seven	(29) Number 4 (3)	(74) full turn fancy	十一月初八 (MOTHER)
(8) " eight	(29) Rubbing & double	(75) one leg step	二月十八 (FATHER)
(9) slide step	(31) change alone	(76) "R" step	九月十五 (PETER)
(10) New step (1)	(32) B step	(77) "R" step.	十一月十六 (ROBERT)
(11) New step (2)	(33) "B" side step	(78) "R" step	十二月廿六 (AGNIS)
(12) change	(34) New L	(79) "K" shake step	九月十 (HING)
(13) changing	(35) waltz step	(80) bicycle step	十一月十六 (ROSIE)
(14) square step	(36) mambo style	(81) 8 step	九月初五 (節父)
(15) Tango step (1)	(37) side step	(82) 4 step	十月廿八 (BRUCE)
(16) " " (2)	(38) straight side step	(83)	
(17) 3 step backward	(39) New side step	(84)	
(18) Banana boat	(40) wave step	(85).	
(19) shake step	(41) circle step	(86)	
(20) starting step (1)	(42) "A" step	(87)	
(21) " " (2)	(43) "B "	(88)	
(22) "Poof" step	(44) "C "	(90)	

Turning step (45)
Turning left (46)
"Jug" step (47)
Duck step (48)
"G" step (49)
"G" step (50)
Samba step (1) (51)
" " (2) (52)
Two full turns (53)
mixed step (54)
basket ball step (55)
men & women (56)
charleston step (57)
Double step (58)
Catch collar (59)
pull step (60)
big circle step (61)
2 step (62)
bend lock & Roll (63)
technique step (64)
one two step (65)
simple step (66)
break step (67)

28

" LEARNING IS A CONSTANT PROCESS OF DISCOVERY — A PROCESS WITHOUT END. "

Bruce Lee

CHAPTER

EVOLUTION
1960-71

At the time of Bruce Lee's return U.S. soil in 1959, Americans had rarely witnessed Chinese martial arts outside of the Chinese neighbourhoods, and even then, it was usually described as 'Karate', whatever the style. However, this decade saw Lee revolutionize completely the perception of martial Arts in the U.S. Lee continued his training in the martial arts, teaching Gung Fu and organizing demonstrations for the local Chinese community. He eventually opened a Gung Fu school in Seattle's Chinatown in 1962, where he not only met his future bride Linda Emery but also James Yim Lee from Oakland.

Over the course of the next few years, Lee's demonstrations, training tours and teaching of celebrity students such as Steve McQueen, James Coburn, Stirling Silliphant and Sy Weintraub caused quite a stir, and Bruce developed his own unique fighting philosophy – Jeet Kune Do.

Opposite top left: Bruce standing outside his first US Gung Fu club premises, located at the junction of Maynard and Weller in Seattle's International district.

Opposite top right: Informal practise with Jesse Glover at his duplex apartment, circa December 1960.

Right: Park practise with Taky Kimura, late 1960.

Left: Bruce sitting between Allen Joe (left) and James Lee (right), during a Christmas visit to Oakland, 1962.

Below left: Photo session with Taky Kimura in Ruby Chow's car park. Photos taken in Autumn 1962 for Bruce's first book.

Below centre: Bruce demonstrating on Ed Parker whilst James Lee looks on during a visit to Ralph Castro's school circa 1962.

Below: Bruce, Ed Parker, James Lee, Ralph Castro.

Right: Car park practise, assisted by Taky Kimura circa 1961–62.

Above: Returning to the USA, August 1963, with Doug Palmer, stopping over in Hawaii and meeting up with Ed Parker at the Chinese Buddhist Temple Hall.

Opposite, top: Posing in Gung Fu attire with Doug Palmer, Hong Kong, 1963.

Opposite, below: Bruce and his father (centre), a Tai Chi practitioner, meeting with fellow enthusiasts at Kings Park, Hong Kong, 1963...

Right: ...Details of the members in the group.

Below: A formal studio portrait of Bruce with Yip Man, his Wing Chun Sifu, Hong Kong 1963.

Below right: Bruce at the Sylvan Grove Theatre, another practice location on the University of Washington campus.

December 30 1963 at
Long Beach Municipal
Auditorium, Long
Beach, California
U.S.A.

Top: Under the guise of a visit with friends to the Rose Bowl Parade in Pasadena, Linda accompanies Bruce on a trip to California, December 1963. From left to right: Linda, Bruce, James Lee and Ed Parker Snr with son Ed Parker Jnr.

Above: Bruce's handwriting on the flipside of the photograph.

Right, above: Bruce outside his University Way premises, which he acquired in October 1963 as both residence and teaching location for the better part of a year.

Right, below: Bruce teaching at the University Way Kwoon, Seattle.

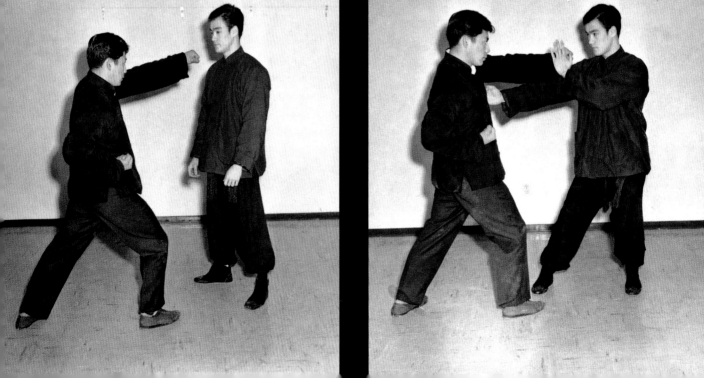

Left: Bruce oversees a class at University Way as Linda demonstrates a counter on Taky Kimura.

Below left and right: Bruce and assisting instructor Taky Kimura pose for a series of promotional photos.

Above left: April 1964 demonstration in Seattle. Linda looks on as Bruce counters an attack by Taky Kimura.

Above right: Linda defends against two familiar assailants. Photo intended as instructional use for the Seattle Jun Fan Gung Fu Institute.

Right: August 1964, Bruce performs at the Long Beach Internationals, assisted by Taky Kimura.

Opposite: After *Longbeach*, and assisted by Dan Inosanto [Above], Bruce continued to tour, intermittently, during August and September 1964, giving controversial demonstrations at Chinese Theatres along the West coast of California.

Below: Alongside his martial art demos, Bruce ralso acted in tandem as bodyguard and dance partner for actress Diana Chang during her promotional tour for Shaw Brothers.

Overleaf: Annotated instructional photo circa late-1964/early 1965, Oakland. Bruce (A) with James Lee (B).

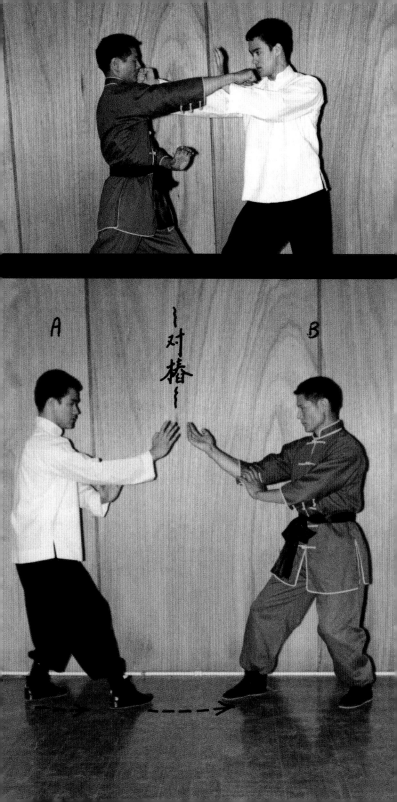

对
椿

"TAKE THINGS AS THEY ARE. PUNCH WHEN YOU HAVE TO PUNCH. KICK WHEN YOU HAVE TO KICK."

Bruce Lee

Above: Rooftop photo session with Robert Chan, Hong Kong, 1965.

Opposite, above: Wing Chun photo session with Yip Man,
Hong Kong, 1965.

Opposite, below: Yip Man holding baby Brandon Lee, Hong Kong, 1965.

Left: Swordplay with Brandon, Barrington Plaza, 1966.

Right: Bruce holds the focus pad for Brandon, Barrington Plaza, 1966.

Above left: Father and son, Palos Verdes, 1966.

Above: Portrait by Chester Maydole, Malibu Beach, 1966.

Left: In action with Dan Inosanto, Malibu Beach, 1966.

Right: Father and son, Palos Verdes, 1966.

"MY STYLE? I CALL IT THE ART OF FIGHTING WITHOUT FIGHTING.

Bruce Lee

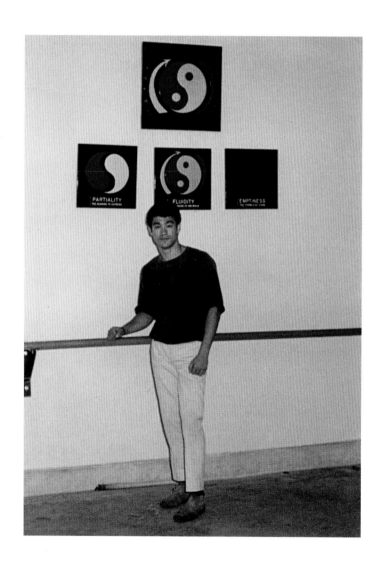

Opposite left: Bruce at the Chinatown LA School, summer 1967, standing in front of the wall signs made by George Lee.

Opposite, above: Left to right: Tony Hum, Bruce, Dan Inosanto at Chinatown LA School, 1967.

Opposite, below: Bruce next to Los Angeles assistant instructor Dan Inosanto, at the opening recruitment lecture for the Chinatown LA school, February 1967.

Above: Jhoon Rhee (right) tournament host and organizer of the Washington DC tournaments with Bruce (centre) announcing and presenting trophies, May 1967.

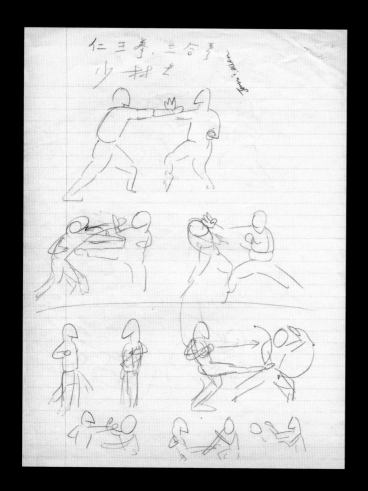

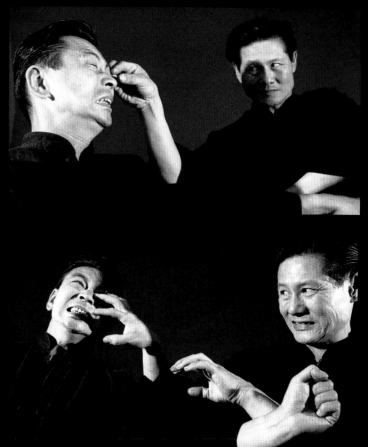

Opposite, top left: Bruce's sketches for a photo sequence featuring James Lee and Allen Joe.

Opposite, top right: James Lee (right) and Allen Joe (left) photo sequence for Bruce's follow-up book project at the Chinatown LA School, July 1967.

Opposite, below: George Lee (left) and Allen Joe (right) pose for additional photos at the Chinatown LA School, July 1967.

Left, above and below: At their Inglewood home, Bruce and Linda pose
for publicity photos, July 1967.

Overleaf: Jhoon Rhee (left) with Bruce, July 1967.

" I FEAR NOT THE MAN WHO HAS PRACTICED 10,000 KICKS ONCE, BUT THE MAN WHO HAS PRACTICED ONE KICK 10,000 TIMES. "

Bruce Lee

Above and below: Bruce demonstrates the close-range power-punch on Oakland student Bob Baker at the Long Beach Internationals, July 1967.

Right: Meeting and greeting during the award ceremony at the Internationals.

Left and opposite: Various photos used to illustrate Bruce's training methods and equipment in Culver City, Los Angeles, 1967.

Right: Final sessions for Bruce's book project in December 1967 and January 1968. Included were a series of "defence-in-the-street" scenarios with the assistance of Dan Inosanto, Ted Wong and Raymond Huang.

Left: Bruce at the International Convention of Martial Arts, organized by *Black Belt* magazine in the Summer of 1968.

Above: Assisted by Dan Inosanto and Ted Wong, Bruce demonstrates the Chi-Sao of Wing Chun for *Black Belt* magazine's 1969 yearbook.

Above and below: Bruce supervising and having fun with James Lee and Ted Wong at a Wing Chun book photo session, April 1971.

Right: From a series of photos taken for Bruce's *Black Belt* magazine article, "Liberate yourself from classical Karate" (published September 1971).

" **I AM NOT TEACHING YOU ANYTHING. I JUST HELP YOU TO EXPLORE YOURSELF.** "

Bruce Lee

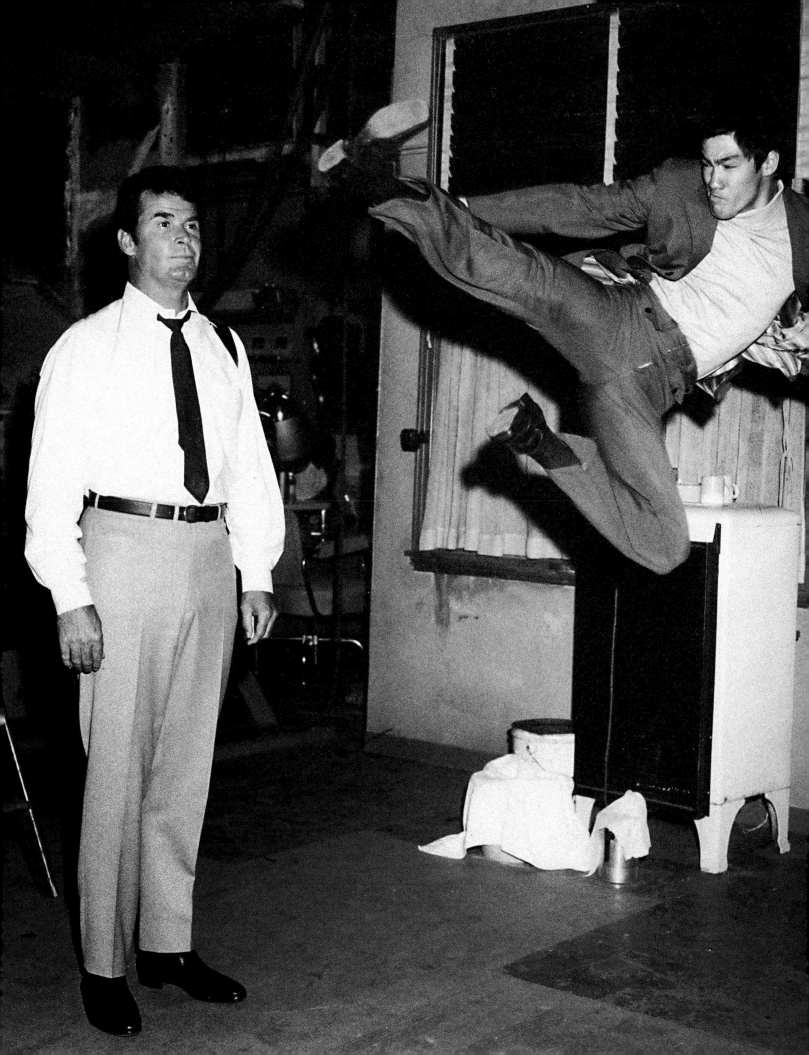

CHAPTER

03

THE HOLLYWOOD YEARS, 1965-70

It wasn't until Lee moved to California in 1964 that his life in movies took a significant turn. Following a successful screen test with 20th Century Fox, it was decided that Lee was the man for the part of 'Kato' in a new TV show, *The Green Hornet*. By March 1966 Lee had relocated to Los Angeles in preparation for the start of filming. The real break came when Stirling Silliphant wrote a screenplay called *Marlowe,* based on an adaptation of Raymond Chandler's 1949 novel *The Little Sister*, and cast Lee as a thug by the name of Winslow Wong. This was a great first appearance for Lee in a major Hollywood movie. MGM was so pleased with his performance that they sent him on a ten-day promotional tour of the country.

Bruce Lee truly believed success in Hollywood would come if only he had a chance to prove his worth. Silliphant had total conviction in helping, but knew only too well the prejudicial barriers the artist would face. Hollywood was not ready for a non-Caucasian lead man, but Lee kept trying.

By 1970, Lee felt there was a chance to finally realize his dream of becoming the first Asian actor to make it into Hollywood in a starring role, and by the turn of the decade to finally develop what he saw as the first true expression of martial art to be portrayed on celluloid – a vision of philosophical genius entitled *The Silent Flute*. But it was not to be, and despite significant support from Silliphant and James Coburn, the project was abandoned.

Right: One of the publicity photos that was used to introduce Lee to the American public as Kato for the *Green Hornet* TV show.

Above: In February 1965, Bruce attended a screen test in Los Angeles which led to his role as Kato in *The Green Hornet* TV series.

"TO HELL WITH CIRCUMSTANCES; I CREATE OPPORTUNITIES.

Bruce Lee

Opposite, left: Bruce reading a script for *The Green Hornet* at home in Barrington Plaza, Los Angeles.

Opposite, right: Bruce alongside his co-star Van Williams who played the Green Hornet (left) and another co-star in the series, Lloyd Gough.

Below and overleaf: The Green Hornet and Kato in action!

Above: Bruce Lee in full flight with Nancy Kwan on the set of
The Wrecking Crew (1968).

Opposite, above: Bruce with Karate champion Joe Lewis, a stuntman
and extra on *The Wrecking Crew* (1968).

Opposite, below: Bruce directing Sharon Tate in one of her scenes.

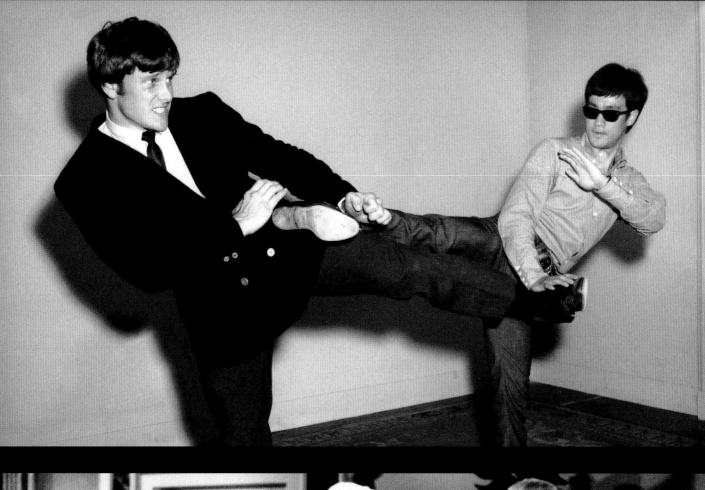

Left: Bruce directing Sharon Tate.

Below: Bruce watches as Kenpo grandmaster Ed Parker demonstrates on Mike Stone as Joe Lewis stands by on set.

Opposite: Bruce teaching Dean Martin, star of *The Wrecking Crew*, the finer points in the art of kicking.

Bruce's character, Winslow Wong, attempting to bribe Marlowe, played by James Garner during that unforgettable scene in *Marlowe* (1969).

I, BRUCE LEE, WILL BE THE FIRST HIGHEST PAID ORIENTAL SUPERSTAR IN THE UNITED STATES. IN RETURN, I WILL GIVE THE MOST EXCITING PERFORMANCES AND RENDER THE BEST OF QUALITY IN THE CAPACITY OF AN ACTOR.

"

Bruce Lee

Winslow Wong dismantling Philip Marlowe's office
with explosive artistry.

Bruce teaches James Garner the art
of board-breaking on set
at MGM studios.

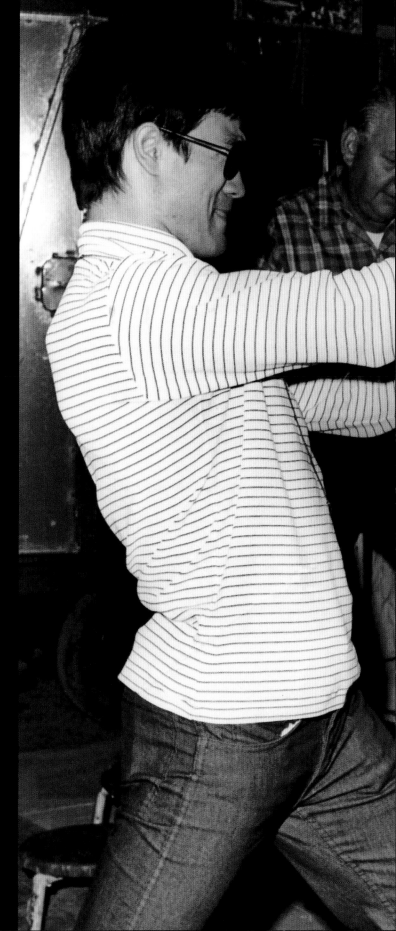

Top: Bruce in the back garden of his Bel Air home, with his pet schnauzer by his side.

Above: Bruce riding horseback with co-star Linda Dangcil in the TV series *Here Comes the Bride*.

Right: Bruce with young Brandon and infant Shannon on his lap.

Opposite: Bruce's mission statement from 1969, inspired by the teachings of American author and impresario Napoleon Hill.

My Definite Chief Aim

I, Bruce Lee, will be the first
highest paid Oriental super Star
in the United States. In return
I will give the most exciting
performances and render the best
of quality in the capacity of an
actor. Starting 1970 I will achieve
world fame and from then onward
till the end of 1980 I will have
in my possession $10,000,000. I will
live the way I please and achieve
inner harmony and happiness

Bruce Lee
Jan. 1969

91

Left: Bruce, alongside Stirling Silliphant, with James Coburn in attendance at Silliphant's Pingree Production offices during script meetings for *The Silent Flute* (1978), 1970.

Above: The trio of Lee, Silliphant and Coburn with a welcoming committee upon arrival in India.

" ART CALLS FOR COMPLETE MASTERY OF TECHNIQUES, DEVELOPED BY REFLECTION WITHIN THE SOUL. "

Bruce Lee

The silhouette of Bruce Lee in the deserts of India,
taken during the visit with Coburn and Silliphant.

Above: Bruce soaring above the sand in the Indian desert.

Opposite: Bruce's handwritten note showing the 'theme'
for *The Silent Flute*.

The Theme :—

Basically this is a story of man's quest for his liberation the returning to his original sense of freedom. Unlike the old west fastest gun alive. the individual is not out to sharpen his tools to destroy his antagonist; rather, his side kick, back fist, hook kick, etc. are directed primarily toward himself. It is because of the self, there arises the foe. When there are no signs [of thought movements] stirred in your mind, no conflicts of opposition take place there; and where there are no conflicts, one trying to get the better of the other. this is known as "neither self nor foe". At its best, the "tool" thus represents the force of intuitive or instinctive directness, which unlike the intellect does not divide itself blocking its own passageway. It marches onward without looking forward or sideways.

The basic problem of a martial artist is known a "psychical stoppage" (It). When he is engaged in a deadly Contest with his antagonist, his mind attaches itself to thoughts or any object it encounters. Unlike the fluid mind in everyday life, his mind is "stopped", incapable of flowing from one object to another without stickiness or cloggyness. He ceases to be master of himself and as a result, his tools no longer express themselves in this suchness. So to have something in one's mind means that it is preoccupied and has no time for anything else; however, to attempt to remove the thought already in is to refill it with another something!

Ultimately, one should be "PURPOSELESS" By purposelessness

Above and opposite: Bruce, teaching a blind detective played by James Franciscus in the pilot episode of *Longstreet* entitled "Way of the Intercepting Fist". A memorable scene.

CHAPTER

04

HONG KONG 1970-73

By the start of 1970, Lee knew that as far as Hollywood was concerned he had a major battle on his hands, and although his close friend Stirling Silliphant was working hard to help, it looked like his future in the States would most likely reside in television work.

The appearance of Bruce Lee on Hong Kong television in April 1970 got the attention of Golden Harvest, a Hong Kong-based movie production company. Manager Raymond Chow offered Lee a two-picture deal and by July 1970, Lee was on his way to Thailand to start filming the first of those two movies, *The Big Boss*.

Between 1970 and 1973, Bruce Lee made five movies for the Golden Harvest studio that would go on to define his global legacy as not only a philosophical genius, but also the king of martial artistry. Buoyed by the international interest in *The Big Boss*, *Fist of Fury*, *The Way of the Dragon* and *Enter the Dragon*, Lee had offers pouring in from many film companies around the world, including old friend and Hollywood star James Coburn, who along with Elmo Williams – one of the top executives from Twentieth Century Fox – proposed to re-ignite *The Silent Flute* project.

By mid-1973, Bruce Lee had started to outgrow the Hong Kong film industry. Hollywood was beckoning and Bruce was confident in his performance in *Enter the Dragon* and had planned his return to the USA. While *Enter the Dragon* did change the world of action cinema and firmly establish Bruce Lee as the first Asian movie superstar, Bruce's death on July 20, 1973, meant that the man himself would never be witness to his own enormous success.

| **Opposite:** Publicity shot, circa 1971.

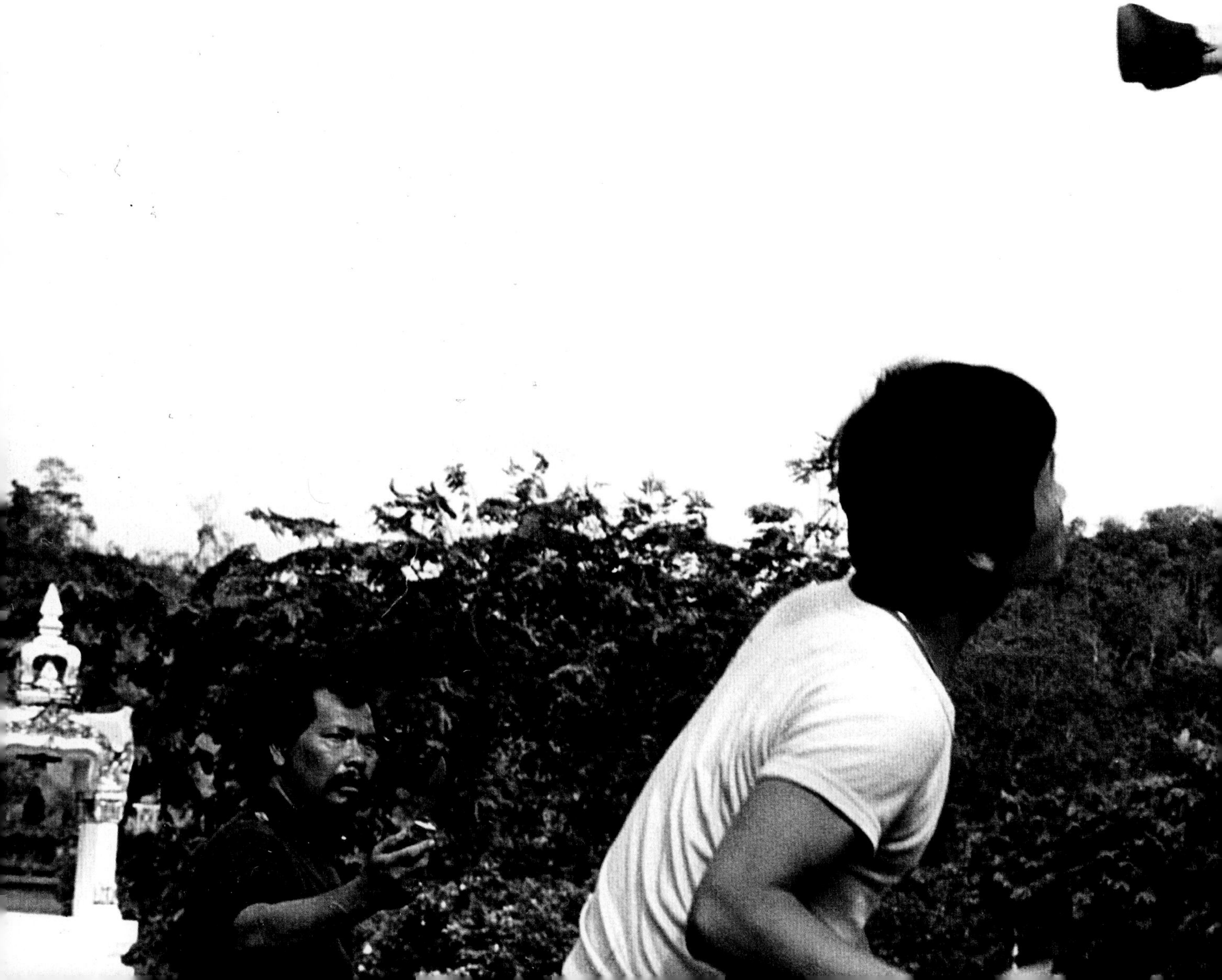

Above: Bruce soaring high, with explosive consequences, from the climatic end fight sequence.

Opposite: Ready to seek revenge against arch villain during the climatic fight sequence in *The Big Boss*.

Overleaf: Publicity photo with co-star Tony Lau Wing.

Opposite top left: Working out a scene at the ice factory in Pak Chong, Thailand, with co-star To Ga-Jing and Wu Chia-Hsiang, *The Big Boss* director before he was replaced by Lo Wei.

Opposite top right & left: Bruce alongside his co-stars during a scene at the ice factory.

Above: Alongside co-star Li Kun as the action kicks off.

Left: From left to right: Han Ying Chieh, Maria Yi, Lo W
and James Tien.

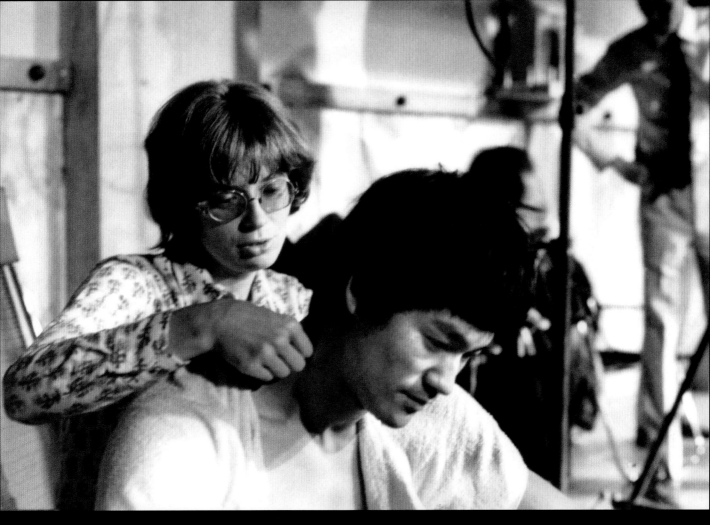

Above: Linda helps out with Bruce's hair on the set.

Left: With Lo Wei during the filming of *The Big boss*.

Overleaf left: Publicity photo with
co-star Tony Lau Wing.

Overleaf, right: Bruce chatting with the wife of director Lo
Wei – and former Shaw Brothers actress – Liu Liang-Hua.

> **"** I HAVE CHANGED FROM SELF-IMAGE ACTUALIZATION TO SELF-ACTUALIZATION, FROM BLINDLY FOLLOWING PROPAGANDA, ORGANIZED TRUTHS, ETC. TO SEARCHING INTERNALLY FOR THE CAUSE OF MY IGNORANCE. **"**

Bruce Lee

" | IF ONE LOVES, ONE NEED NOT HAVE AN IDEOLOGY OF LOVE. | "

Bruce Lee

Above: Bruce and Linda at the gala premiere of *The Big Boss*,
November 1971.

Right: Bruce during the filming of *The Big Boss*.

" **A FIGHT IS NOT WON BY ONE PUNCH OR KICK. EITHER LEARN TO ENDURE OR HIRE A BODYGUARD.** **"**

Bruce Lee

Appearing on TVB with Robert Baker to promote the premier of *The Big Boss* (1971), October 22, 1971.

Left: *Fist of Fury* publicity photo on the set with Peter Chan Lung (left) and Max Lee Chiu-Chun (right).

Above: Memorable scene with co-star Paul Wei Pin-Ao.

Above left and right: Bruce talking to Lo Wei during a break from the publicity photo session for *Fist of Fury*.

Left and right: *Fist of Fury* publicity photo with co-star and student Robert Baker.

Left: Making Peter Chan Lung and Max Lee Chiu-Chun eat paper, a scene from *Fist of Fury*.

" TO ME, THE EXTRAORDINARY ASPECT OF MARTIAL ARTS LIES IN ITS SIMPLICITY. THE EASY WAY IS ALSO THE RIGHT WAY, AND MARTIAL ARTS IS NOTHING AT ALL SPECIAL; THE CLOSER TO THE TRUE WAY OF MARTIAL ARTS, THE LESS WASTAGE OF EXPRESSION THERE IS. **"**

Bruce Lee

Left: Bruce arrives in Hong Kong, early 1972.

Below: Relaxing in his office in Hong Kong, circa December 1972.

Right: Playing around with weights in Hong Kong, c. December 1972.

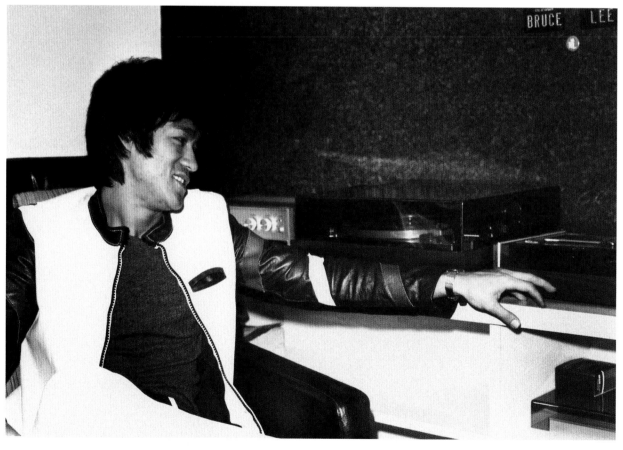

Above: Location shoot at the Coliseum, Rome, with Chuck Norris and assistant director Chi Yao-Chang.

Right: Bruce shows the mob boss, played by Jon Benn, the power of the Little Dragon.

Left: Bruce wielding not one but two sets of nunchaku as he single-handedly takes apart the Italian thugs in the movie.

Right: Bruce kicking his way out of trouble in *The Way of the Dragon*.

" THE LESS EFFORT, THE FASTER AND MORE POWERFUL YOU WILL BE. "

Bruce Lee

ONE SHOULD BE IN HARMONY WITH, NOT IN OPPOSITION TO, THE STRENGTH AND FORCE OF THE OPPOSITION.

Bruce Lee

Bruce displaying his lightning-fast kicks against Bob Wall (**opposite**) and Hwang In-shik (**this page**).

Overleaf: Rehearsing and directing the movie's climatic fight sequence with Chuck Norris.

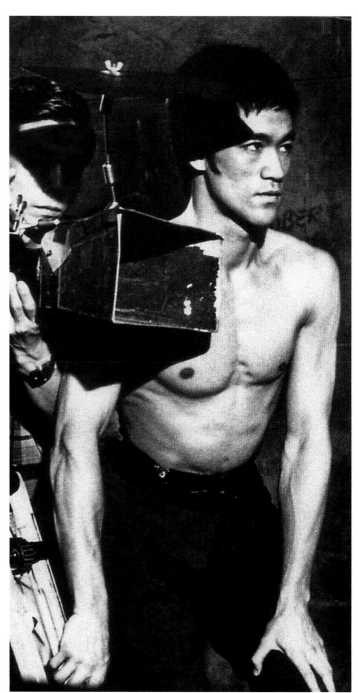

Working hard on the set of *The Way of the Dragon*. It was one of the biggest ever martial arts movies and was hugely influential in opening up that genre to a larger audience than ever before.

Publicity photos with seven-foot three-inch-
tall friend and student Kareem Abdul-Jabbar.

Publicity photos with co-stars James Tien and the towering Kareem Abdul-Jabbar.

Facing friend and student Dan Inosanto
in their on-screen nunchaku battle.

The trio of Bruce, Chieh Yuen and James Tien in original footage shot for *Game of Death*.

The fight scene between Bruce
and Hapkido expert Ji Han-Jae.

A visit from Warner Bros. producer Fred Weintraub (second from right) during the production of *The Game of Death*

ALWAYS BE YOURSELF, EXPRESS YOURSELF, HAVE FAITH IN YOURSELF, DO NOT GO OUT AND LOOK FOR A SUCCESSFUL PERSONALITY AND DUPLICATE IT.

"

Bruce Lee

Left: Publicity photo with friend Unicorn Chan on the set of the movie *Fist of Unicorn* (1973), circa July 1972.

Above: On the *Enjoy Yourself Tonight* show on Hong Kong's TVB with host Tam Bing Man, September 3, 1971.

Right: Bruce and Brandon on TVB's *Operation Relief* show with host Josiah Lau, June 24, 1971.

Below: Demonstrating on the RTV *Golden Hour* show, April 1970.

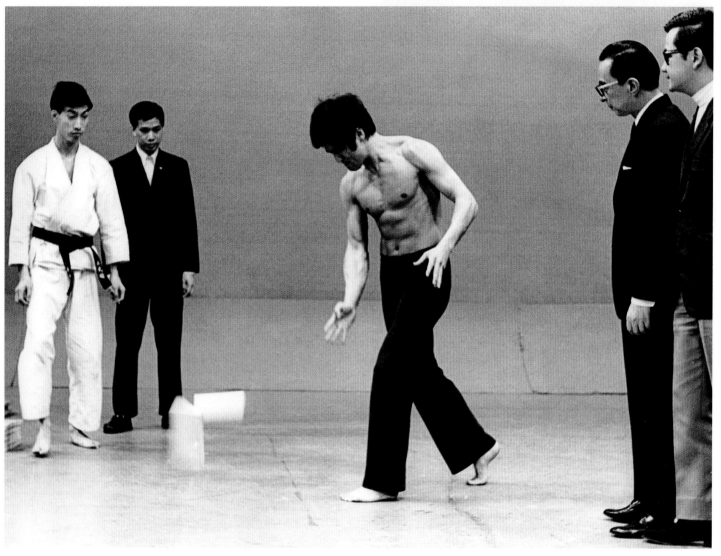

Left and bottom: Bruce alongside Golden Harvest executive Leonard Ho at Kai Tak airport in Hong Kong, on his return to the U.S., September 6, 1971.

Below: Bruce and family return to the airport on October 16, being greeted by Maria Yi and Raymond Chow.

Right: Bruce in an experimental classical period costume at Golden Harvest studios, circa March 1972.

Left: The opening fight at the Shaolin Temple against Sammo Hung.

Above: With the head abbot of the Shaolin Temple (played by Hong Kong movie veteran Roy Chiao Hung) in a scene originally omitted from the movie, but reinstated two decades later for the home video/DVD release.

Left: Publicity shot for the movie.

All opposite, top left: Director Robert Clouse calls "Action".

Top right: Bruce overseeing the filming on set next to Warner Bros. cinematographer Gil Hubbs.

Centre left: Talking to co-star and arch villain of the movie Shih Kien.

Centre right: Scaffolding "Chinese style".

Below left: John Saxon discussing the script with director Robert Clouse and producer Fred Weintraub.

Below right: Bruce talking to Raymond Chow on set.

Overleaf: Bruce took an active role behind the camera as well as in front of it.

> **"WHEN ONE HAS REACHED MATURITY IN THE ART, ONE WILL HAVE A FORMLESS FORM. IT IS LIKE ICE DISSOLVING IN WATER."**
>
> *Bruce Lee*

Bruce about to take apart the villainous O'hara, played by Bob Wall.

Bruce in action during the cavern fight sequence in which he wields several weapons including the staff, *escrima* sticks and what would become his signature weapon, the nunchaku.

> **ALL IN ALL, THE GOAL OF MY PLANNING AND DOING IS TO FIND THE TRUE MEANING IN LIFE: PEACE OF MIND.**

Bruce Lee

Left: Bruce rehearsing the big battle towards the end of the film (above) and the same sequence during filming (below).

Right: Bruce knocking down one of his multiple opponents in classic fashion.

Overleaf:
Above left: Facing veteran Hong Kong actor Shih Kien as the infamous Han. This photo shows Bruce resting on a support so the camera can get a close-up in slow motion of his foot kicking Han in the head in the flying-kick sequence.

Below left and right: Bruce before and after his clash with the claw of Han.

Right: Promotional photo from the hall of mirrors where Bruce Lee faces Han in the climax of the movie.

Above and right: Publicity photographs taken in Hong Kong, December 1972.

Above: Bruce appears at his old school, St Francis Xavier, to present awards, March 1973.

Right: Alongside singer/actor Samuel Hui at the Chinese New Year celebrations in February 1973.

Overleaf left: Alongside Shaw Brothers director Chor Yuen during a visit to the Shaw Brothers studio, circa Sept 1972.

Overleaf right: Period-costume test photo at Shaw Brothers, April 1973.

Left: A bearded Bruce Lee at the New Year celebrations, February 1972.

Above: At Kai Tak airport meeting James Coburn as the Hollywood star and friend visits Hong Kong, April 1973.

> ## "IF YOU LOVE LIFE, DON'T WASTE TIME, FOR TIME IS WHAT LIFE IS MADE UP OF."

Left: Meeting James Coburn at Kai Tak airport in Hong Kong, April 1973.

Right and below: Costumed photo-shoot at Shaw Brothers Studios in Hong Kong, circa April 1973.

" ULTIMATELY, MARTIAL ARTS MEANS, HONESTLY EXPRESSING YOURSELF. NOW, IT IS VERY DIFFICULT TO DO. I MEAN, IT IS EASY FOR ME TO PUT ON A SHOW AND BE COCKY AND FEEL PRETTY COOL OR I CAN SHOW YOU SOME REALLY FANCY MOVEMENT. BUT, TO EXPRESS ONESELF HONESTLY, NOT LYING TO ONESELF, AND TO EXPRESS MYSELF HONESTLY, NOW THAT MY FRIEND, IS VERY HARD TO DO. "

Bruce Lee